Chris Hudson is an experience
author, based in the West Midla
adults and children alike. This
Chris' concern for the happiness and health of the children under
his care, and as a result of several memorable summer camps
at Shugborough Outdoor Education Centre in Staffordshire. The
stories are based on real-life incidents, but the characters are
fictitious and should be treated as such.

TRURO DIOCESAN
BOARD OF EDUCATION

Text copyright © Chris Hudson 2004
Illustrations copyright © Ann Kronheimer 2004
The author asserts the moral right
to be identified as the author of this work

Published by
The Bible Reading Fellowship
First Floor, Elsfield Hall
15–17 Elsfield Way, Oxford OX2 8FG

ISBN 1 84101 327 7

First published 2004
10 9 8 7 6 5 4 3 2 1 0

Acknowledgments
Unless otherwise stated, scripture quotations are taken from the
Contemporary English Version of the Bible published by HarperCollins
Publishers, copyright © 1991, 1992, 1995 American Bible Society.

A catalogue record for this book is available from the British Library

Printed and bound in Great Britain by
Bookmarque, Croydon

Stories
to keep you
healthy

Chris Hudson

Acknowledgments

With grateful thanks to the following
for making this book possible:

Alison Farnell and all at the Stapleford Centre.
Sue Doggett, my very understanding editor at BRF.
The staff of Shugborough Outdoor Education Centre,
Staffordshire, for putting up with myself and my pupils
for so many years.

The past pupils of Year 6 at Greysbrooke School, Staffordshire,
who have made my life over the last few years so...
well... interesting.

Many of the events portrayed in this book are based on real-
life incidents, but all the characters are fictitious and should
be treated as such. No resemblance to any real-life person is
intended—with the exception of Mr Les Stewart, whose
contribution to my pupils' outdoor education experience over
the years has always been immensely valuable.

Teacher's page

What? A book about Religious Education and Health?

There's more to Health Education than Science and PE lessons.

Science schemes contain lots of excellent investigations for children about discovering how their bodies work, but they can be rather limiting. We are not just mechanisms that need to be understood and maintained with the sort of regime that you would use to look after a car. We feel. We grow. We develop an image of ourselves and a collection of likes and desires that affect how we feel and how we grow. That image influences our choices of food, exercise, and everything else. 'Health' has to be a bigger issue than simply knowing about how your body works.

Physical Education is also important, but it's limiting to encourage children simply to feel good about taking exercise. Are they encouraged to reflect on what it feels like to compete in a match, or to reach a personal best in an athletic event? These issues are interesting in themselves (especially to boys), and deserve some space in the school curriculum. Certain children dislike PE lessons because it reminds them of what they *can't* do—should we class them as 'special needs', and go out of our way to support them in feeling good about their own bodies? Discuss!

Our medical understanding of the human body has advanced in leaps and bounds over the last century, but we aren't necessarily happier or wiser, despite improved medical treatment. Some of the most 'developed' societies in our world also have the highest suicide rates. I am personally very grateful to the pharmacist who can sell me a prescription that reduces pain, or the physiotherapist who can teach me a set of exercises to mend a strained back, but a sense of well-being *has* to involve more than pain relief.

We need to relate modern discoveries about our minds and bodies to older ideas about what makes a person unique and special. That is why the stories in this book use ideas found in the Christian Bible. The peoples of the past lacked our modern insights into disease and healing, but many of them seem to have led happy, long and well-adjusted lives. Three thousand years ago, the writer of Psalm 90 alludes to a normal human lifespan of seventy years, and eighty if someone is particularly lucky. So much for life in the past being nasty, brutish and short!

Perhaps, despite all our knowledge, they can still teach us a thing or two.

Contents

Introduction: Trapped!

Five days out of school! David couldn't believe it. Five days *not* doing all the normal lessons. It was amazing! He'd heard about the school camp for years, and now he was finally going AT LAST! His mum had packed him an *enormous* rucksack full of clothes and sweets and everything he'd need for a week away from home—and then he'd found the first problem. He couldn't carry it.

'Come on!' said Dad. 'Try!' David tried. Then his dad picked up the rucksack, put the straps on David's back, tightened them to fit, and let go. David fell over. After Dad had finished laughing, they repacked the bag, taking out a lot of things that didn't need to be there. ('Does he need *ten* pairs of under-pants?' Dad called out as Mum found something else to do.) In

the end it was all sorted, and on Monday morning they all headed off to school in the car to catch the coach at 9.15am. There were lots of other parents, some looking a bit tearful. All the bags were loaded, the goodbyes were said, and then it was all on to the coach. At last! A whole week's holiday. Nothing to do but mess about with your friends for a whole week. Heaven!

It was after they arrived at the centre that David started to change his mind. They'd just met Mr Stewart, the instructor, who was wearing a purple tracksuit and sounded like a sergeant-major.

'Right then!' he shouted. 'These are your tents! I'm going to explain how you put one up, and then you are going to put up your own tents at the same time. We'll do it all bit by bit, so you'll have to listen closely. Do you know what will happen if you don't listen closely?'

Twenty-five silent faces stared back blankly.

'You don't? Then I'll tell you. Your tent will fall down, and if it's raining, you will get wet! Is that clear?'

Twenty-five heads nodded.

Mr Stewart demonstrated how to unfold the tents and peg out the groundsheet, then sent the group off. David was puzzled. How could it be a holiday if they told you what to do? The others who'd been before hadn't talked about this. Soon everybody was sorting out the mysteries of tent poles and A-pieces and guy ropes and mattresses, then fetching their bags to go inside.

Great, thought David. Now we can play.

'Right then!' shouted Mr Stewart. 'Well done! You've got about ten minutes to get yourself over to the classroom, and then we'll be starting the first activity. Is that clear? Well, off you go!'

David crawled into the tent to find a chocolate bar. He had a horrible feeling that something was wrong. This wouldn't be a holiday after all. It was all going to be like school, but different. There were *no* computer games, *no* television, and there would be no chance of escape. He was trapped—in Camp Doom.

Diet and exercise

Everything God created is good.
And if you give thanks, you may eat anything.

1 Timothy 4:4

When God says that something can be used for food,
don't say it isn't fit to eat.

Acts 10:15

We live in a country where nearly everybody can eat what they want, when they like. Supermarket shelves are positively *heaving* with so many types of food. God wants us to enjoy our food and be thankful for it, and there's so much to choose from—but we can spoil it if we get very fussy about our likes and dislikes.

I don't like the food

Somewhere, a bell was being clanged.

'It's one o'clock, everybody!' yelled Mr Davidson. 'Time for lunch! Line up in your teams by the dining hall!'

The whole class left their tents in dribs and drabs, trudging up the field towards the long low building by the road. Food! What would it be like? Ben lined up with the others in C team, behind a letter painted on the tarmac.

'Are you all here?' asked Mr Stewart. Each team counted themselves several times to make sure.

'Lottie's still coming!' said one girl from Team B.

'Well, your team will have to wait until she's here!' said Mr Stewart. 'Team A, as you go in, please wipe your feet and take off any hats. As you go in, you will be told where to sit, and that will be your team table for the rest of this week. In you go!'

The children filed into the dining room, to be greeted by the wonderful rich smells of cooking food. They sat down where Mr Stewart told them, chattering excitedly and pointing at the photos and artwork on display on the walls. Ben could see pictures of children rock-climbing, paddling canoes and shooting arrows at a target. There was even a photo of some kids standing next to an igloo that they'd made. Snow? Here? Soon they were all sat down, and, with a metal spoon, Mr Stewart hit a large bell hanging from the ceiling, then waited for silence.

'Now then, you have two choices for your lunch today—it's pizza or sausages, and you can choose from chips and other vegetables when you are served. When it's your turn, you will need to get up, collect your food tray on the left, and then make your choices from the food that's on offer. Don't forget to say "please" and "thank you" to the ladies who serve you. Take what you want, but eat what you take. Is that clear?'

They all nodded, and lunch began.

⚙ What kinds of food do you like? Why?

Ben felt a little uneasy. Pizza? Sausages? He only liked the ones they had at home that his mum cooked, or the ones that came from the takeaway. It was soon his table's turn, and, with a shuffle of chairs, they were lining up. The food trays had compartments like the ones some children had for school dinners. Oh no! This was school dinners, wasn't it? He didn't *have* school dinners. He had 'sandwiches'—only it wasn't sandwiches. At school, his mum sent him with a lunch box containing a packet of crisps, a chocolate bar, a chocolate mousse and some pop in a flask. That was it. *And now they were going to feed him school dinners!*

It was his turn. 'Pizza or sausages?' asked the lady. Ben didn't know. Both looked totally *wrong*, nothing like anything he had at home. *His* pizzas were round, and these were cut in rectangles. The sausages were long and thin, and he was used to them being short and fat. It was *all wrong*.

⚙ Are there any foods *you* don't like? Why?

'Come on, there's other people behind you!' said the lady, smiling. 'Pizza or sausages?'

He had to choose. 'Sausages,' he said miserably. Two long sausages were plonked on his tray, and he moved on to get some chips and beans. Soon he was back at the table with the others. They were tucking in. These were all his friends, but he now felt so alone. They couldn't see that the sausages were wrong, and the chips were the wrong shape as well. The beans tasted funny too. Why was everybody eating them?

He felt he needed a drink, and noticed there was a water jug on the table. Water? No squash or pop? Just water? He didn't drink *just* water. This was awful. Everything was wrong, but his friends were eating everything and drinking *just water*. What could he do?

Sarah was sitting opposite. She was the first to notice. 'Ben! You're not eating!'

'I don't like the food. It's all wrong.' He was hoping for some sympathy, but it didn't come.

'Oh, right!' she smiled, eyes wide open. 'Can I have yours, then?'

Ben was speechless with surprise, but he nodded. Soon, his sausages and chips and beans were being taken by Sarah, who shared them out with Paul next to her. Ben's plate came back empty. He realized that he wasn't going to have any lunch now. He slumped back in his seat, then cheered up when he remembered that there were some chocolate bars and biscuits in his suitcase. He could have them later. Would they last him for the whole week? Ben didn't know.

Mr Stewart rang the bell again, and waited for silence.

'Now then, I hope you've enjoyed your meal. When your whole table has finished, please give all your trays and cutlery to one person who will take it up to put on this trolley for washing up. Someone else will need to take up the jug and cups. Then your whole team has to make sure that the table is wiped down.

When you are ready, you all sit and put your hands up, and I'll come and tell you to go. You stand, put your chairs in, then leave by *that* door (he pointed) where there are some muffins waiting for you. Take *one* each *only*, and then you can eat it outside. Please put all the paper cases in the bins provided. Then you will have some free time until your next activity. Is that clear?'

✪ **What sorts of jobs do you have to do at meal times?**

And so it was done. Mr Stewart had to shout at the children of one table who all trooped up carrying their plates instead of giving them to just one person, but it all seemed to work out.

Ben trudged outside clutching his muffin. Was that it? Was that lunch? This place was terrible. He nibbled the muffin. It had currants in it. He didn't like currants. He only liked chocolate chip muffins. He took a mouthful, then threw the rest in the bin.

'Hey! I could have had that!' yelled David, who was next to him. Ben ignored him. David was a greedy pig anyway.

It was a long afternoon. His tummy rumbled several times when they were out canoeing, and he felt a bit weak. The evening meal was meat pie with mashed potatoes, and he had some of that, but left a lot of the pastry. It was too hard and crunchy. The pudding was an iced bun, and he ate that—but at the end, he was still feeling hungry. Later that evening, he tucked into his precious store of biscuits. There was only one packet. Would they last him all week?

Next day came the long walk. They'd all had to order their sandwiches from the kitchen, and Ben ordered cheese. They were all packing their satchels when the lunches arrived. Ben's heart sank. The sandwiches were made with *bread rolls*! He *never* ate bread rolls! They were the *wrong shape*! He packed them anyway, along with some crisps, an apple and a chocolate bar. Of course, he wasn't really going to eat the apple. It was the wrong colour, a bright green. What did they think he was? A rabbit?

Why do you think they included an apple with his lunch?

Other children have said...

'...so he has a balanced diet...'

'...to keep him healthy...'

'...to make him strong...'

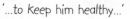

The walk started. The whole party headed off across the field to a track that took them under a bridge, past a fence, then through some woodland. Soon, they had crossed a road and were on the Chase, a large natural forest that was once kept by King Henry VIII for hunting deer.

'How far are we going?' asked Ben.

'Oh, about ten miles,' replied Mr Davidson.

'TEN MILES?'

'Well, maybe twenty. We'll see how far we get. Have you brought your sleeping bag?'

Ben realized he was only joking. Adults! Typical! The walk began—every now and then they stopped and Mr Stewart would tell them something about the wildlife in the area. He even sent them on a 'fungi hunt', looking for strange varieties of mushrooms and toadstools. They were just coming out of the forest when the first 'challenge' happened.

'Right then!' said Mr Stewart, pointing up a hill. 'This cleared area is a fire-break that runs all the way up this slope and then down again in a large circle! Your challenge is to run up and round it in the shortest possible time. There will be team points for the fastest times—so get ready!'

It *looked* easy. They dumped their satchels in a pile, then lined up. 'GO!' Twenty-five pairs of legs started running up the hill. Pretty soon, some of them had slowed to a trot and others were walking. 'IT'S A RUN, NOT A SUNDAY AFTERNOON STROLL!' shouted Mr Stewart. Ben was walking, breathing hard. His legs felt all trembly, like jelly. They'd *never* felt like *that* before! After what seemed like an age, he found himself at the top along with a few others, and decided to try to run down. His legs felt so weak! Left, right, left, right—he was trying not to fall over. Soon, he was back.

'Well done, Ben!' said Miss Acton, as he collapsed in a heap at the bottom. 'Get your bag, then! We're off again!'

The trail led up another hill, then down on to another track which took them towards a stream. 'Here's your second challenge!' roared Mr Stewart. 'Your challenge is to hop across these stepping stones to the other side.' Soon, a whole line of children were hopping across, a few falling in, but most of them making it across and keeping dry. David fell in, but that wasn't unusual. (He probably did it on purpose.) When it was Ben's turn to hop, he felt all weak again. Hop, hop hop, whoops! He didn't fall in, but it was close. Once across, he suddenly felt *so* tired. How much further did they have to go?

'Is it lunch time yet?' he moaned.

'Lunch time? It's only half past eleven!' snorted Mr Davidson. Ben nibbled on a chocolate bar anyway. He was feeling all hot and cold at the same time. Then it started raining—so they all had to put on their waterproofs. Ben was feeling really cold now. That's odd, he thought. I don't normally feel that in the rain.

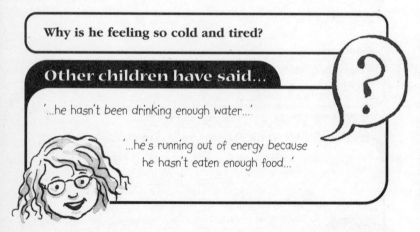

Why is he feeling so cold and tired?

Other children have said...

'...he hasn't been drinking enough water...'

'...he's running out of energy because he hasn't eaten enough food...'

They finally found the place for lunch, and everyone dug into their satchels. Ben ate his crisps and his other chocolate bar, then started thinking hard. The cheese roll *was the wrong shape*, but he was hungry. Then he had an idea. He could, if he

shut his eyes, imagine it was normal white sliced bread, couldn't he? It was a new idea, but he was hungry, and new ideas sometimes come when you're desperate. Pretty soon, the roll was eaten. That left the apple, but it was green. He only liked red apples, but... what if he shut his eyes again? He tried a bite, and it worked. The apple tasted a bit different and sharper, but it wasn't as bad as he expected.

Have you ever tried a food and found it wasn't as bad as you expected?

Other children have said...

'...when I tried a cheese flan. It tasted good!'

'...my first chicken curry! It was hot, it burned my mouth, but it was nice!'

'...my first bite of the meat pie we had for school dinners!'

?

Now he was thirsty—and the only thing to drink was *just water*. His mouth felt dry, but there was no choice. *Just water* it would have to be. He poured the water from the flask into his cup, and drained it in one swallow. Hey, that was good. He poured himself another.

This was strange. He had made a discovery. When he was hungry, he found he could eat and drink things he didn't normally like. He wondered what they were cooking for dinner tonight. He was actually looking forward to it, this time.

Did you know?

Your body needs a mix of certain foods to make it work—and, like a car, it will start to 'break down' if it doesn't get all the things it needs. That's why you can start to feel faint if you go without food for a certain time, because you are running out of energy.

The main food groups are:

- **Carbohydrates and Fats**—to give you energy and keep you warm.
- **Proteins**—to enable body cells to repair themselves, and to build new cells.
- **Fibre**—to give your digestive system something to get a grip on.
- **Vitamins and Minerals**—to provide the basic materials so that your body can create all the other very complicated chemicals it needs to work.

If your normal diet lacks any of these groups, then some things won't work so well.

Water is also important, however you drink it. Your body

needs a steady supply of fluid to do all the jobs it does, especially when digesting food, and you also lose *a lot* of water just by sweating and going to the toilet. You need to keep taking in fluids *all through the day* to keep the right balance of fluid in your body. Without it, you'll start feeling tired and dopey!

❖

Thinking time

Are there any foods that you dislike? Try to think why that is. Could it be because of:

- The colour or shape?
- It has new, unfamiliar flavours?
- It reminds you of something else you don't like?

Do you think these are good reasons?

Many children prefer foods that have been heavily processed in factories. These are often made with added chemicals that make the food look better (or stay fresher for longer), but aren't actually much good for us. Why do you think adults buy these products?

Prayers

Father God, thank you for food, for all the wonderful tastes and flavours that come to us from around the world. Help us not to be fussy when we find something new on our plate. Thank you for all the people who spend so much time preparing our meals. Amen

Father God, we have so much food in this country, when there are many children in the world who have so little. Please guide our leaders to share the world's food with others in a fair way. Amen

Thinking time activity

Our eating likes and dislikes are often first based on what we see. Create a blindfold food-tasting quiz where someone has to try to identify types of food from taste alone. It can be harder than you think! Start by identifying types of fruit that have been cut into similar-sized chunks.

Make sure that your hands and food preparation surfaces are clean before you start, and that you have the permission of your parents or carers before you raid the larder or fruit bowl. Also, make sure that your 'tester' doesn't suffer from food allergies.

An alternative approach is to use food colouring to stain different foods the 'wrong' colour and see whether people are willing to try them. It can be quite weird to be faced with eating a green pancake! Again, ask for permission before you start, and ensure that all food is prepared safely and hygienically.

Self-image and personal responsibility

Only fools would trust what they alone think, but if you live by wisdom, you will do all right.

Proverbs 28:26

Fools show their stupidity by the way they live; it's easy to see they have no sense.

Ecclesiastes 10:3

Have you noticed that there are some people who always seem to have accidents? Sometimes, those accidents happen because we don't think before doing something.

In fact, it can become a bit of a habit not to think about what could happen. It can even be dangerous. God gave us all a mind, which we can choose to use—or not. See what Petra does with hers.

The strange case of the exploding toilet

Petra couldn't believe it. One minute ago, she had been dashing into the washrooms and shutting the toilet cubicle door because she was 'desperate'. She'd shut the door, taken down her joggers and plonked herself down on the seat. Then, there was this almighty crack, and the whole thing fell over in pieces. Water started pouring everywhere, and she was stuck on the floor with her face rammed up against the wall. What had happened?

It was all too scary. She got to her feet, pulled up her joggers and staggered out, leaving a trail of soggy footprints. Her teacher was sitting outside in the sunshine, reading a book.

'I've just smashed the toilet!' declared Petra, with tears in her eyes.

'You did *what*?' Miss Acton put the book down.

'I sat down on it and it… it exploded!' she said, trembling.

'It… *exploded*? I've *got* to see this.' Miss Acton had a strange look on her face as Petra led her teacher in to show off her handiwork. Water was pouring out of a broken pipe and streaming across the floor towards a gutter. Miss Acton took a quick look into the cubicle at the shattered toilet, then came out. 'Petra, are you all right?' she asked.

'Y-y-yes! W-w-will I have to pay for any d-d-damage?'

Miss Acton's face was a strange mix of expressions. She seemed to be thinking of several things at once. 'Petra... you go and wash your hands, and I'll go and tell one of the centre staff. Have you got that?'

It was only when Petra had disappeared from sight that Miss Acton started laughing hysterically. 'It EXPLODED!' she shrieked. Things like this 'happened' to Petra all the time. It was nearly always 'somebody else's fault', and Petra always looked very sorry afterwards. But this was the first time she'd ever heard of a girl blowing up a toilet! In the staff room, the teachers were all howling with laughter at the news.

'We've *got* to stop giving these kids baked beans!' shouted one. Everybody roared.

Petra was very worried. Do you think it was fair for the teachers to laugh afterwards?

Other children have said:

'...not really, but it was sort of funny!'

'...yes and no. She couldn't hear them, so it wasn't hurting her feelings...'

'...I would have laughed too!'

Why was it *always* Petra? She didn't know. Things just... sort of happened like that. When they went out canoeing after arriving on Monday, she fell in not once, not twice, but *nine* times. *Nine times!* 'You've spent more time in the water than out of it!' said the instructor. It had been funny the first time, but then it kept on happening.

Petra kept messing about, trying to bump her canoe into the others. She'd look over one shoulder, lean back, and (surprise, surprise!) the whole canoe would tip over, and she was swallowing river water again. When she wasn't falling in, she was ending up stuck in the side of the riverbank.

'Why aren't you listening?' asked the instructor, rather amused. 'I told you how to stop capsizing, but you keep on doing it! Why do you keep trying to bump into the others? Do you *like* being upside down?' Everyone had laughed, but Petra didn't think it was funny. She preferred it when *she* was making the jokes.

How do you think Petra is feeling at this point in the story?

Other children have said:

'...a bit mixed up. Things aren't going right for her...'

'...it's like a game that's going wrong...'

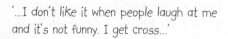

'...I don't like it when people laugh at me and it's not funny. I get cross...'

On the first night, Petra was laughing and joking with the others in her tent at lights out. She'd brought lots of biscuits and crisps, and when the other children fell asleep, she started scoffing. It must have been twelve o'clock before she decided to snuggle down. It felt odd trying to sleep with a face covered in crumbs.

It was Tuesday, after the long walk, when the toilet exploded. Of course, everyone laughed at that, but it was such a stupid

thing that she didn't mind, once she'd calmed down and found out that she wouldn't get into trouble. The staff said it was probably cracked anyway, so that made it all right… in a way. It made her the centre of attention again, and she liked that.

That evening, she'd spent more time eating late into the night. It only stopped when Miss Acton heard the rustle of crisp packets at 11.00pm, and had demanded she hand them over *now* through the tent flap. Petra felt it was so unfair. She was so hungry.

On Wednesday she fell off a picnic table near the dining hall. Of course, Petra wasn't *supposed* to be standing on the table, but she'd jumped on top of it for a laugh, then fell off and banged her head.

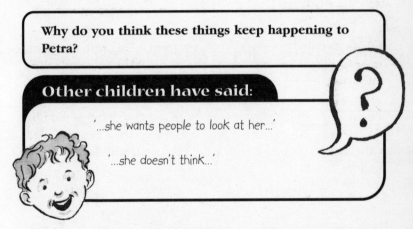

Why do you think these things keep happening to Petra?

Other children have said:

'…she wants people to look at her…'

'…she doesn't think…'

Miss Acton came to check she was all right after the picnic table incident. 'Petra,' she asked, 'do you know that you're your own worst enemy? You want everyone to notice you, even if it means doing really stupid things to make them look. Do you really *want* them to laugh at you? Do you really *want* to be the class clown?' There was no answer to that sort of question.

That evening, after the lights were out, Petra felt hungry again, and started reaching into her bag to find another packet of biscuits. The wrapper rustled.

'Petra! Will you give it a rest?' That was Ravinder talking from inside her own sleeping bag. 'Do you *have* to keep us awake while you stuff your face? Some of us want some *sleep*!'

'What's wrong?' asked Petra, mystified.

'You haven't shared any of your stuff, have you?'

'Do you want a biscuit, then?'

'NO! It's just… why are you so selfish the whole time? You're not the only one here, you know! Just let us sleep!' There was a rustling as Ravinder wrapped herself up further.

Petra couldn't see what all the fuss was about. They were only biscuits, and she was hungry! *What* was wrong with that? She was *always* hungry. It was as if there was a big hole inside her wanting to be filled, and the only way to do it was by being the centre of attention, or by stuffing herself with food.

On Thursday, there was the business with the spoon. At the end of a meal, Petra had decided to try catapulting a spoon over the heads of the other people on her table. Then the others joined in. Soon there were spoons flying all around the table—and Petra had ended up getting one smack in the eye. Her left eyelid had puffed up all red. For a few minutes, the staff had been thinking of taking her to hospital.

'Will I have to go home?' she asked Miss Acton, rather sadly.

'No, but I've got to try to explain something to you. Are you listening?'

Petra nodded.

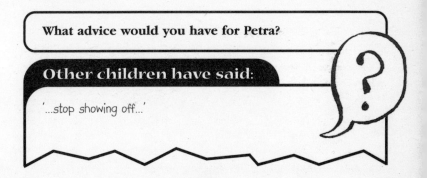

What advice would you have for Petra?

Other children have said:

'...stop showing off...'

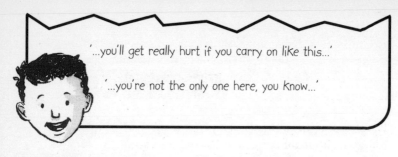

'...you'll get really hurt if you carry on like this...'

'...you're not the only one here, you know...'

'Petra, there's two ways to behave,' said Miss Acton. 'You can be sensible, or you can be stupid. "Sensible" is when you think about what you're going to do before you do it. "Stupid" is when you just do anything without thinking. You've been acting in a stupid way all week, and you've got hurt. Does that tell you something?'

Petra didn't like the sound of *that*. 'The toilet wasn't my fault!' she protested.

'Pardon? Who was sitting on it at the time? Nobody else I know has *ever* smashed a toilet just by sitting on it! Were you messing about in there?'

'No!'

'Petra, we've *seen* you do stupid things all week. So why should we believe you now, when you say you weren't doing something stupid while we *couldn't* see you?'

Petra went quiet. She didn't have an answer to that.

Miss Acton kept talking. 'Petra, you don't need to act as if you only had half a brain. Think! If you want everyone to laugh at you, then just carry on! But I don't think that's the *real* Petra. The real Petra's a lot more thoughtful and caring. I've seen that some-times. Why not let us see her a bit more often? Why not just try being sensible for the next 24 hours? That way, *you'll* get home safe and sound, and *we* won't have to make a hospital visit.'

Petra nodded sadly. This camp hadn't turned out the way she wanted. She thought it would be five days of messing about, but she'd ended up feeling rather battered by everything that had happened. If there was a hole inside her wanting to be filled, it wasn't getting filled up like this.

❖

People sometimes do all sorts of strange things without thinking about it. It can be because they're feeling sad or un-happy. What do you do? Could you take these feelings and do something more positive with them? Why not try:

- writing them down in a diary
- talking about it to somebody
- creating a poem that explains how you feel
- drawing it in cartoons
- deciding to make someone else happy instead

Can you think of any more?

Prayers

Father God, I don't like to get hurt. Help me to think before I do something so silly that it hurts me or hurts someone else. Help me to take responsibility for my own actions. Amen

Father God, I'm thinking about (name a friend of yours), who keeps getting into trouble and can't seem to stop it. Help me to be a good friend for them. Amen.

Look at some newspaper stories, and cut out those stories that show some-one who wasn't thinking before they did something. ('Road accidents' would be a good place to start.) If they had thought, how would the story have ended differently? Make the cuttings and your comments into a poster with the title 'Think first!'

Homesickness, relaxation and managing stress

Can worry make you live longer?

Luke 12:25

If you fall, your friend can help you up.
But if you fall without having a friend nearby,
you are really in trouble.

Ecclesiastes 4:10

What sorts of things scare you? Different people will say different things. There can be fantasy fears, such as ghosts and monsters, which usually come from watching too much TV. There are other things that can be much more scary—like being away from home, or missing the people who love you. Jesus said he would *always* be there for his friends, but he also told them to care for each other—because where two or three of them were gathered together, then *he* would be there too, in the background, encouraging them.

In this story, Jackie gets very frightened. Try to see how it starts—and what happens next.

I want to go home!

It was the moment Jackie had been dreading. Ever since they'd arrived, the children had been making themselves busy, putting up tents for the school camp, having meals and doing activities, but now it would be different. It was getting dark, and tonight would be the first night she'd ever spent away from home *and* away from her mum and dad.

Jackie had always been like that, ever since she was small. She'd go on holiday with her parents, but had always found it hard to settle at night, even when they were all sleeping in the same room. This was all horribly different! She would be sleeping in a tent with Stephanie and Paula! She felt the air growing colder, and shivered. Home was thirty miles away. She wanted to be there, in her own bedroom under her own duvet.

What do you think she is frightened of?

Other children have said...

'...the dark...'

'...she's in a strange place...'

'...it starting to rain, and everything getting wet...'

What's the worst thing likely to happen?

Other children have said...

'...the tent could fall down...'

'...bugs could come into the tent...'

'...burglars could come!'

'Come on, girls,' said Miss Acton. 'Clean your teeth and get sorted for bed!'

But I haven't got a bed, thought Jackie. I've only got a sleeping bag and a thin plastic mattress. She took her wash-bag and went to clean her teeth, but she knew it was only putting off the dreaded event. Soon, she was walking back through the darkness to her own tent. There were excited whispers and flashes of torchlight as everyone was settling in. A loud shriek from Tracey's tent told everyone that Tracey was having a good time. Jackie crawled into her tent to find the others already wrapped up inside their sleeping bags and talking about boys.

'Where've you been?' asked Stephanie.

'Cleaning my teeth,' answered Jackie. She was going to be sleeping *right next* to these people. They weren't members of her own family or *anything*, and she was sharing a tent with them! She got into her nightclothes and wriggled down inside her own sleeping bag while the others carried on gossiping. The ground underneath felt hard and cold.

The others carried on talking and playing with their torches, while, outside she could hear the teachers walking around and telling the different tents to 'hush'. There was loud laughter from another tent (probably Tracey's) and then the wind started to pick up, rustling the flysheet of the tent. Would it rain tonight? It was forecast. Imagine if their tent fell down in the rain! She thought of the tent cloth falling on her face and tangling her up so she couldn't breathe—and shuddered. No, it was silly. She looked at the zips that fastened up the 'doors' to the tent. They *wouldn't* jam up, would they?

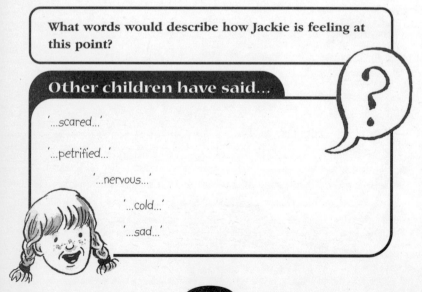

What words would describe how Jackie is feeling at this point?

Other children have said...

'...scared...'

'...petrified...'

'...nervous...'

'...cold...'

'...sad...'

?

But just suppose it *did* fall down. What would happen then? Would anyone ever know? She snuggled up tighter in her sleeping bag and tried to think of something else. It was hard. Her parents would just be going to bed now. She wished she could phone them, but Mr Davidson had said that phoning home only made people feel *more* homesick. It was too late to go home now, she knew that. Bit by bit, she grew more sleepy, although she was still worried. The whispering voices of the others seemed to be drifting away...

'WHERE'S THE KEY?' She sat up and yelled it again. 'WHERE'S THE KEY! HELP!' Stephanie and Paula were suddenly awake. They had been asleep for about an hour before the shouting started.

'Jackie!' called Stephanie.

'What's wrong?' asked Paula.

'I CAN'T FIND THE KEY!' shrieked Jackie. 'I WANT TO GET OUT!'

'It's a *tent*, silly!' said Paula. 'It doesn't have a lock!'

'I WANT THE KEY!' she shouted again.

Mr Davidson was out the front, now. 'What's wrong, girls?' he asked.

'It's Jackie!' said Stephanie. 'She's just sat up and started yelling things!'

'WHERE IS IT?' yelled Jackie, desperately.

'Jackie, are you all right?' asked Miss Acton. She was pulling back the zips of the tent flap and shining her torch inside. Jackie looked terrified. She was staring around wildly at all of them. And she was still asleep.

Have you ever talked or walked in your sleep? What happened?

Other children have said...

'...I got up in the middle of the night and went to sit on the toilet. My dad found me there and I was still asleep, and the lid was down!'

'...my parents say I'm rude to people in my sleep, but I can't remember any of it!'

'...my sister went sleepwalking, and woke up to find herself curled up on the bookcase!'

'Let's get her out and calm her down,' said Mr Davidson. Jackie was taken over to the staff room, wrapped in a blanket and given a warm milky drink. She was fully awake now at last. What had been going on? She felt so confused. Why was she out of bed? They explained it all to her.

'Were you having a nightmare?' asked Miss Acton.

'I don't know...' she replied sadly, 'but I just want to go *home*!'

They talked it through with her, and she agreed to go back to the tent and try to sleep.

'Will she settle down now?' whispered Mr Davidson.

'If she doesn't, we'd better get a rubber mallet,' snorted Miss Acton.

Nothing else happened that night, but in the morning Jackie felt really terrible. She knew that *something* had happened last night, and that she had been crying out, but it all seemed to be a million miles away now. The sun was out and people were getting ready for breakfast. She felt really silly. The others giggled a bit when they gave her the full story, and she laughed along with them, but she wondered what it would be like later on.

❂ **What is it about the darkness that can make people feel nervous? Can you think of ways to help someone with that fear?**

Today, Tuesday, was the day of the long walk on the Chase, and she really enjoyed it. Ben didn't seem to be having a good time, but she didn't know why. Peter was his same old moaning self. Everything was normal—but when they were back, she had that awful sense of doom washing over her again. It would be getting dark soon. It would be *just* like last night. She was nervous again.

After the evening activity, there was a bit of free time. Some of the boys went off to play football. Stephanie and Paula went to watch, then came back laughing. It was then that Mr Davidson got out his guitar. He sat on a bench by the tents, just strumming away. Miss Acton was with him, flicking through a songbook. Jackie went over to look. The songbook was all handwritten.

'Where did you get it?' she asked.

'I wrote it,' he replied, strumming away. 'Many years ago, I started collecting my favourite songs and writing them down.

Every now and then, I add a new one.' Miss Acton let Jackie take
a closer look. The handwriting was a lot larger and clearer than
the sort he used to mark her creative writing, but maybe he had
more time when he was writing this! There were songs by the
Beatles, the Beach Boys and lots of other musicians from the
1960s and 1970s.

She stopped at a page. 'I know this one! It's in the charts now!'

'That's because a good song keeps coming back,' he replied, smiling. 'They always do! Come on, let's sing one!' Together, they tried a few Beatles songs, then some of the others. Stephanie and Paula joined in. Soon, they were adding dance moves and actions. Jackie had *never* done anything like this before! It was fun! A small crowd was gathering around the bench, some with torches because it was too dark to see without them.

'Let's do *Summertime Blues*! It's by Eddie Cochran!' Morris shouted.

'WHO?' they all shouted.

'Eddie Cochran! He was one of the first rock-and-rollers! He's really *cool*!'

And so it was that Morris found himself doing a solo of *Summertime Blues*, with everyone clapping along and cheering at the end. Jackie had never seen him like this before. Coming to camp had made Morris into a different person—or was he like that anyway?

It was time for cocoa. Mr Davidson packed away his guitar and they all trooped up to the canteen. It was completely dark now, but Jackie didn't mind. After all, there was nothing out there in the dark that wasn't there in the day. Later, as they settled down in their tents, she could hear Morris singing again, 'Sometimes I wonder what I'm a-gonna do, but there ain't no cure for the Summertime Blues…'. She smiled again. Maybe she would sleep better tonight. She wasn't alone now.

What things made the difference for Jackie on Tuesday night?

Other children have said...

'...she knows the people around her now...'

'...she doesn't feel the cold in the same way...'

'...she knows that the darkness isn't really very different to the light...'

'...she feels safe now...'

What does that tell you about coping with fear?

❖

Thinking time

What is fear? The person who doesn't fear anything can be a very scary person to be with, because they don't *know* what's dangerous. Fear can be useful, because it helps us to see trouble coming and do something about it.

- Can you think of times when fear has been useful for you?
- Have there been times when it has spoiled things for you?

Thinking time activity

What things worry you? Take the time to think and list all of them, no matter how silly they seem to be. Now cut them out and sort them into groups headed 'Fantasy Fears' which are made up, and 'Real Fears' which really *could* happen. Then look at the 'Real Fears' group. Would it help to discuss them with someone you can trust? It's amazing how talking about your fears can help you to handle them! Some people also find it helpful to draw or model the things that frighten them. Would it help you?

Dealing with alcohol

Don't be a heavy drinker.

Proverbs 23:20

It is not clever to get drunk! Drinking makes
a fool of you and leads to fights.

Proverbs 20:1

Don't destroy yourself by getting drunk,
but let the Spirit fill your life.

Ephesians 5:18

In this country, we can get very confused when talking about alcohol. Many adults use alcoholic drinks, like wine, beer or spirits, for celebrating special events like weddings, or they might just drink them to have a good time. We also see lots of adverts encouraging people to drink this beer or that spirit, especially at the party season. On the other hand, we also know that alcohol misuse spoils the lives of thousands of people every day, by causing accidents and illnesses. Some people (called alcoholics) become so addicted to it that they can't get through a day without having 'just one more'. It's all very confusing. See how the girls in this story deal with it.

The night of the bottle

'Where did you get it from?' asked Sarah on Tuesday afternoon.

'It was on the Chase. Do you remember when we were exploring among those trees, looking for fungi? There was this little shelter that somebody had made, and I looked inside. *Look* what they left behind!' Tracey held the strangely shaped green bottle up to the light. It was about half full. The label said 'Cherry Brandy', but she didn't have a clue what it tasted like.

Sarah looked outraged. 'Tracey! You're a nutter! You're not going to drink *that*, are you? Imagine what'll happen if you get caught! What was it doing there, anyway? It could be poison!'

'Poison?' Tracey's eyes lit up and she gave her friend an evil grin. 'Then I'm going to feed it to you in the middle of the night and you'll DIE! HA! HA! HA!' Sarah squeaked in outrage, then giggled. She liked the way Tracey said and did silly things. *She'd* never dream of doing it, but she sort of liked having someone who did as a friend.

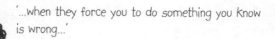

Other children have said...

'...when they do things you don't like...'

'...when they do something, and then if you don't do it they call you a woosie...'

'...when they force you to do something you know is wrong...'

Tracey put the bottle back in her rucksack. 'Anyway,' she smirked, 'it means we can have a real midnight feast in the tent tonight! What do you think?'

Sarah grinned. Why not? That's what friends were for. They were here on the school camp to have a good time, and that's what *adults* did when *they* wanted a good time. They had a few drinks, and they all laughed. She'd seen her parents do it at parties. They also took her older brother down to the pub for his first legal drink when he was eighteen. They even let Sarah have a few sips of wine at meal times when she asked, which showed there was nothing wrong about it. She wondered what Michelle would say when they told her. They'd have to tell her because she was sharing their tent, so she had to be in on the secret.

Do you think there's anything wrong with drinking alcohol?

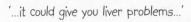

Other children have said...

'...it can make you feel very ill...'

'...it could make you drunk...'

'...it could give you liver problems...'

Why do you think there are legal restrictions about buying and drinking it before you are eighteen years old?

Other children have said...

'...if you're younger, it could do something to your body...'

'...it could affect your health if you're young...'

It was after tea time when Tracey showed Michelle the bottle in the tent, just before they all went off to their evening activities. Michelle didn't say very much, but just got up and walked out. That was odd. She didn't normally say *nothing*. In fact, Mr Davidson often had to tell her off in class for saying too much. Never mind—it was time for everybody to go to the indoor climbing wall to get fitted up with helmets, and it was all too busy to have a private talk.

After the climbing, they all trooped back to their tents to sort out their hair (those awful helmets!) and fetch their mugs for cocoa. In the dining room, Sarah grinned at Tracey, and Tracey grinned back at Sarah across the room and raised her cup like somebody saying 'Cheers!' with a pint of beer. Sarah giggled to herself. It was so funny! Tonight was going to be a riot! They were the first girls back to the tents *and* the first to get their teeth cleaned and pyjamas on, before zipping up their tent. Michelle was already in and inside her sleeping bag when they came back. They were going to have a *party*!

What do you think is going to happen next?

Other children have said...

'...they'll drink too much and get drunk...'

'...they'll do bad things...'

'...the teacher might see them...'

Gradually, all the tents went quiet as the children settled down for the night. (They were settling more quickly after a couple of nights out in the open.) Soon, Sarah could hear the footsteps of the teacher on patrol going away. She knew there would always be a teacher around, but they would be left alone in their tent now, just as long as they kept quiet. She was trying hard not to giggle.

'Are you ready?' whispered Tracey. She turned on her torch and found the bottle. The stopper wasn't too firmly stuck, and

she soon had it out. A faint fruity smell wafted around the tent. 'Mmmm!' whispered Tracey. 'Just the way I like it!' She raised the bottle to her mouth, and took a sip. 'Beautiful!' Then she took another, and giggled. 'Hey everybody! I'm drrruuunkk!'

'Give me some!' asked Sarah. The bottle was passed over. Sarah had a sip. It tasted like weak blackcurrant pop. Was that what brandy tasted like? She took another swallow. Wow! This was it! They were having a real drink in their own tent, miles from home. It felt so wonderfully wicked. Tracey let out a large burp and they both started giggling out loud. They couldn't stop! It was all so funny! Tracey let out a wild scream of laughter and Sarah started howling along with her.

There was a voice outside. 'Oi! You two! Will you *please* keep your noise down!' Mr Davidson was calling from inside his own tent. 'Some of us are trying to get some sleep! Pack it in!' Oh dear—he sounded like he meant it too. Oh well—party over for now. Sarah snuggled down inside her sleeping bag. Then she started thinking. Was *this* what being drunk was really like? She'd tasted little sips of wine that made her feel a little giddy, but the brandy actually wasn't doing that at all. Was brandy different to wine? She knew it was served in big glasses, but the adults never drank very much at one go. Something wasn't right.

She also wondered why their noise had disturbed Mr Davidson in his tent ten metres away, but not Michelle, who was now asleep right next to them. She hadn't joined in with the drinking, and hadn't stirred once. In fact, she had been tucked up and was almost asleep when Tracey and Sarah had arrived at the tent. Wait a minute… Sarah nudged Michelle.

'Michelle! Are you all right?' No answer. 'Michelle! Wake up!' Nothing. Something really was wrong. Oh no. She'd seen something like this on *Casualty*. There was a little boy who'd drunk some stuff from a bottle in his uncle's drinks cabinet, and the paramedics had brought him into the hospital because he was in a coma. Alcoholic poisoning! That was it! They couldn't wake him up! She tried shaking Michelle, but it made no difference. She nudged Tracey. 'Tracey! I'm frightened!'

'What?' It sounded like Tracey had fallen asleep too.

'It's Michelle! She won't wake up! I think she had some brandy! She's been poisoned!'

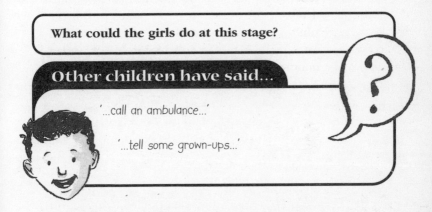

What could the girls do at this stage?

Other children have said...

'...call an ambulance...'

'...tell some grown-ups...'

Tracey was fully awake now. 'Poisoned? We've got to do something! Make her sick! Quick!'

'Sick? How do we do that?'

'I don't know! Our dog makes itself sick by eating grass!'

'I can't stuff grass down her throat!'

'We'll have to get Mr Davidson!'

'We'll get in trouble!'

'We can't let her die! I'll go!' There was a hurried putting on of tracksuit bottoms and trainers and an unzipping of the tent flap. *Why* was it so hard to do something at night in a tent when you were in a hurry? Sarah heard Tracey stagger outside—then there was a loud thump and the tent shook. Silence.

'Are you all right?' whispered Sarah.

'It's all right, I tripped over a guy rope! I'm going now!' The sound of Tracey's footsteps disappeared into the night. Sarah felt so alone. Then something moved beside her.

'What's happened?' asked Michelle.

'Tracey's gone to get help,' replied Sarah.

'Why? Is anyone hurt?' asked Michelle.

'We thought you were poisoned… by the brandy.'

'Oh… that. No.'

'Are you all right? We couldn't wake you up.'

'I'm always like that. My mum says I could sleep through an earthquake. Has she really gone to get Mr Davidson?'

'Your mum?'

'No, silly. Tracey.'

'Yes.'

'Oh.'

More footsteps were coming. Mr Davidson had arrived along with Miss Acton, who had been roused from her tent as well. Tracey was nearly crying, half-sobbing as she tried to explain what had happened. Torch beams shone through the flap into the tent, and Mr Davidson put his head in to see what was going on.

'Oh… Michelle! Are you all right?'

Michelle smiled, her eyes squinting in the bright light. 'Yes, Mr Davidson.'

'What's happened? Tracey's been talking about some brandy from a bottle. Have you had some?'

'No.'

'Where is it?'

Michelle reached over to Tracey's bag, pulled out the bottle and handed it over. 'It's all right, there isn't any brandy in it,' she yawned. 'I poured it away when nobody was looking, and put some blackcurrant pop in.'

'You WHAT?' asked Sarah.

'When?' asked Mr Davidson.

'Why?' asked Miss Acton, who had just arrived.

'Just before supper. I didn't want them getting drunk. I know what it's like.' She yawned. 'Can I go back to sleep now?'

No, she couldn't—not yet. All three had to put on their coats and come over to the staff room to explain what had happened. Mr Davidson wrote it all down and explained it to Mr Stewart, the member of the centre staff on night duty. The bottle was emptied out into a glass jug, and they sniffed the contents.

'It looks like blackcurrant pop to me,' said Mr Stewart.

'It *is* blackcurrant pop,' said Michelle. 'I put it in there from my flask.' Mr Stewart and Mr Davidson took a sip. They looked at each other and nodded. It *was* blackcurrant pop. He turned to Michelle.

'Why didn't you just come and tell us, if you were worried about your friends?'

She spoke quietly, and her face went very serious.

'Because they'd say I was a goody-goody and a spoilsport who didn't want to have any fun. But they don't know what that stuff does.' She was angry now. 'I've seen my sister when she's been drinking. It's horrible! She says horrible things and she gets into fights and I hate her!' The room was silent now. 'My mum had to take her to hospital once, but they said they didn't want to know, and couldn't help unless she came back sober. Then they'd try to help.'

There was a long silence, finally broken by Mr Davidson. 'I... I think it's time to go to sleep now. Nobody here has drunk any brandy, have they? Nobody here feels giddy, or anything?'

The three girls shook their heads.

'Right then. So there's no harm done, as far as I can see. I think we need to talk more about this tomorrow, when everybody's had some sleep. Do we think that's a good idea?' The children and other adults nodded. 'Tracey... Sarah... what Michelle has talked about is private. I don't want you talking about it to anyone else. Is that clear?'

They agreed, and were sent back to their tent. Sarah noticed Michelle hanging back and talking with Miss Acton, who gave her a big hug before sending her on to join the others at their tent.

As they were zipping themselves into their sleeping bags, Sarah had a thought. If there was no brandy in the bottle, then why did she and Tracey act so drunk and feel so silly?

It didn't make sense. Didn't people need to get drunk to have a good time? She'd think a bit more about that—tomorrow.

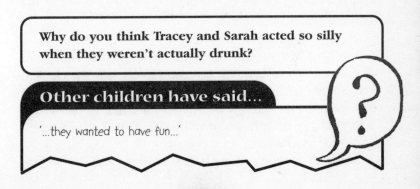

Why do you think Tracey and Sarah acted so silly when they weren't actually drunk?

Other children have said...

'...they wanted to have fun...'

'...they thought they were drinking alcohol, and they thought it would feel like that...'

'...you can get hyper from fizzy drinks and pop...'

'...they wanted to act cool so they felt giddy...'

What does that tell you about having fun?

Other children have said...

'...you can have a good time without alcohol...'

Did you know?

The current law says that children under the age of eighteen must *not* be allowed to buy or drink alcoholic drinks in a public place. Sixteen-year-olds can buy or drink beer or cider in a public place *if it is served as part of a meal*. None of this covers what happens at home, where children may be served alcohol by their parents, who must take responsibility for them.

Over one thousand young people under the age of fifteen are admitted to hospital every year with alcohol poisoning.

They all need emergency treatment—and some die.

After drinking alcohol, you are far more likely to have an accident, because it slows your judgment. Because of this, there are strict laws about not driving a car or motorcycle after drinking alcohol. Some people are also more likely to get into fights and get hurt.

Long-term heavy use of alcohol can lead to many health problems with the heart, the liver and the stomach.

❖

Thinking time

What sorts of things would make *you* want to drink alcoholic drinks before you were the legal age? Would you drink one if you were offered it:

- by a friend at a party?
- by a friend or relative at a family celebration?
- by a parent when you were having a meal together?
- by a friend when you were out in the park?

What would be your reasons in each situation?

Prayers

Father God, as I get older I will have to learn to make more choices for myself about what is right and what is wrong. Help me to judge wisely, and not just go along with what my friends say. Amen

Father God, thank you that we can have so much fun in life. I don't need things like alcohol to have a good time, I can just do it anyway. Thank you! Amen.

Thinking time activity

Find some adverts for alcoholic drinks in magazines. Look at the images and ideas. How are they trying to persuade people to buy? What sorts of people are they trying to impress? Do you think they give the whole picture about what happens when you drink alcohol? Why do you think that is?

Now create an advert that tries to persuade young people not to drink alcohol before they reach the legal age. Could you make it as impressive as the magazine adverts? (There may be graphics on your computer that could help you.)

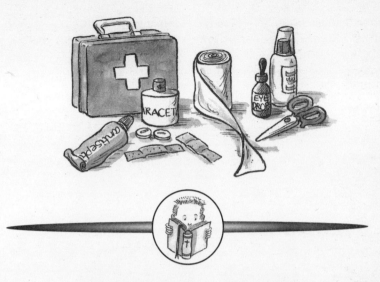

Anger and accidents

Too much pride brings disgrace;
humility leads to honour.

Proverbs 29:23

Don't make friends with anyone who
has a bad temper.

Proverbs 22:24

Some people lose their temper very easily. It can be over really silly things like who kicked the ball in a game of football—but if we lose our tempers, then people's feelings or bodies can get hurt. These are the careless 'accidents' that come from taking things just that little bit too far. If we think we are at the centre of our own little universe, it can make us very selfish. Sometimes, that has consequences...

The clocks

Simon hated hospital waiting rooms for all sorts of reasons. For a start, he hated the waiting. The clocks seemed to be designed to travel *really slowly*. He'd look at the big clock by Reception, then look at it later, and the stupid thing would have hardly moved at all. Once you are stuck in the waiting room, you are trapped for ever. There's no escape. All you can do is wait... and wait... and hope that, just maybe, you might fall asleep. Or die. Or do something that turns your brain off from the long waiting.

Simon was stuck here with Philip. Phil was his best friend, but something had happened at camp and they both had to be taken to hospital. Simon was all right, there was nothing wrong with him. It was Phil who had something wrong with his ankle, and a bruise that was going more blue by the minute.

'Do you think they'll have to do anything at the hospital?' Simon had heard Phil asking Mr Davidson in the minibus.

'I just don't know, Phil,' replied their teacher, 'I'm not a doctor. It looked all right this morning, but that ankle's starting to look rather nasty. We've got to get it checked out in case there's something worse than a bruise. Does it still hurt?'

Phil bent over and touched the dark swollen patch above the heel, and winced. 'Yes.' He didn't like hospitals, and he was rather frightened of pills or needles.

Have you ever been in a hospital waiting room? What was it like?

Other children have said...

'...there was nothing to do...'

'...all I could do was sit and wait...'

'...it's boring and annoying and horrible...'

?

○ **How do you think Phil is feeling?**

The journey by minibus hadn't taken long. Mr Davidson and the two boys had rushed into the Casualty department at the hospital, waited ten minutes for someone to ask them a few silly questions about name, address, date of birth and that sort of thing, then they waited another 27 minutes before another nurse came to have a closer look. Since then, they'd been waiting *over an hour*. Simon looked down at his own hands, clenching them and unclenching them. This was stupid. It had all been an accident. They were meant to be doing archery this afternoon, but he and Phil were stuck here, bored out of their brains. *Phil* was the one who was sick! Why did *he*, Simon, have to be here?

He knew the answer to that one. *He'd* been the one who'd done it. They were playing football just after lunch, and Simon had performed an excellent sliding tackle. He was rather good at those, and really enjoyed seeing the players collapse in a heap as his feet took the ball away from them while tripping them up. He'd been angry at the way the other side were winning so easily, so he'd decided to make them stop *no matter what*. Phil

had yelled in pain as he'd fallen over, and Simon had laughed. *That* would teach them.

He'd forgotten about it until later, when Mr Davidson asked Phil why he was limping. That was when Simon had to explain what had happened, and say sorry, and be told that if there was another incident like this then he'd be *sent home*. Grown-ups always said things like that to Simon, but he didn't think they meant it because they said it so often. He just had this way of getting worked up about things, and then other people ended up hurt. Sometimes, he'd go all hot-blooded and angry when he was arguing, and an adult would tell him to go away and calm down. He could 'flip' very easily.

That afternoon, they'd all gone climbing, but then Phil asked if he could sit down because his ankle was hurting, and the instructor had looked closely at him. The grown-ups had started looking closely at the ankle, which was starting to swell up and turn blue. When the climbing session had finished, Simon kept an eye on the grown-ups. They were whispering among themselves, stopping every now and then to look at Phil, and then at Simon. This did not feel good.

In a few minutes, the instructor took another look at Phil's ankle—and then said he ought to go to hospital.

Mr Davidson had come over to talk to Simon. 'You caused the accident, so I think you ought to come along and keep Phil company.' Then Simon had started crying, saying it was an accident and please don't tell his mum. Now, in the waiting room, he didn't know what to think. His eyes ranged over the posters that dotted the walls, telling people that 'No Smoking' was allowed and 'Please be Patient, the Medical Staff are Working as Fast as They Can'. In the corner, a television flickered, showing an American police programme. Simon wondered what was going to happen to him.

What words would best describe what Simon is feeling now?

Other children have said...

'...nervous...'

'...frightened...'

'...guilty...'

What if Phil had to stay in hospital? Would his parents have to come? Would he have to have an operation? The injury looked nasty. Simon shivered. He didn't know what happened if your ankle was broken. He knew a little about how bones worked, and how they support your body and give the muscles something to pull against. Would Phil be able to walk after this? Would he still be able to play football? He'd never be a good striker with only one good working leg. Simon felt sick inside.

If Phil had to stop playing, it would all be *his* fault and he knew it.

It wasn't fair. It was only a game. They were only messing about. It wouldn't have happened if Phil hadn't come at the goal like that. They were playing hard, going for the ball like he'd seen on television. They'd been told time and time again to

'Take it easy, it's only a game, there's people dying in this world for not having enough to eat, and you're getting worked up over a game of football!'—but it hadn't mattered to him. It hadn't mattered until this. If he could have turned the clock back, he would have done, but he couldn't. The clock just kept ticking forward, very, *very* slowly.

On the TV, a police car sped along the freeway after the bank robbers. Would he have to talk to the police? They wouldn't put him in prison, would they? No, that was silly, that was for when you did things on purpose, and they didn't put children in prison, did they? He didn't know. Simon didn't *know* how bad it all was.

Have you ever been in a situation like this, when you don't know what is going to happen? What's it like?

Other children have said...

'...I had hit my sister and said it was an accident, but it wasn't—I did it on purpose, but I didn't want to get into trouble if it was really bad...'

'...I once threw a stick and it hit my uncle in the eye. The others were seeing if he was hurt, and all I could do was stand there and watch...'

⚙ **What do you think is going to happen here?**

Then the nurse appeared, bearing a clipboard and a smile, asking if Philip could be brought through into a cubicle. They all went through some double doors that swung shut behind them,

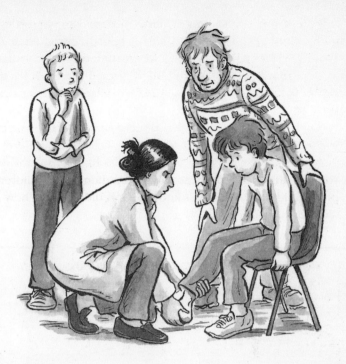

then through some curtains into a small room. The nurse said that the doctor would be along shortly, and could you please wait here. There was one chair, and Phil sat down on it, while Simon and Mr Davidson stood nearby, not saying anything.

They waited another ten minutes. Two cubicles along, a little girl was crying and her mum was telling her to be brave. Simon stared out of the window, looking at nothing, and hoping that it would all go away.

Then a doctor swirled in, wearing a white coat and holding the same clipboard that the nurse had been using. The nurse was looking at the notes. Philip looked tearful. Then the doctor asked a few questions, and asked if she could have a look at the foot. She seemed to have gentle hands.

'Does this hurt?' she asked, gently prodding different parts of the foot and ankle and the area around the bruise, then spoke to Mr Davidson.

'Are you his teacher?' He nodded. 'There's nothing broken, but it's a bad sprain, and he'll have a bit of a bruise for a few days. We won't need an X-ray.' She looked down at Phil. 'It's a good thing you're still a bit bendy around the joints! We'll strap it up, and I'll give you a prescription for some liquid paracetamol, to take away some of the pain.'

'So I won't have any needles?' Phil looked anxious.

'No, no needles.'

Phil started crying with relief, and so did Simon. Mr Davidson looked relieved too.

The whole examination had taken less than five minutes.

The doctor wrote out a prescription, and Mr Davidson took it with the boys to the pharmacy, where the medicines were given out. While they were waiting for the pharmacist to sort it out, Mr Davidson used his mobile phone to call the camp and ask if someone could come and pick them up soon. Simon felt like walking on air. Phil was all right! *He'd be all right!*

Why is Simon happy?

Do you think Phil is feeling the same?

It was raining when they came out to the car park, but it didn't matter to Simon. He felt like jumping a dozen cartwheels and yelling 'YES!' at the top of his voice. He felt safe again, and that life could go on as normal. How long would it be before the minibus arrived? He couldn't wait to get back. They'd be playing football, and he wanted to join in again.

It was tea time when they arrived back at camp. The other children were really pleased to see them, and they were soon swapping stories about the afternoon. Simon was a bit miffed at missing the archery, but there was still the evening to look forward to. Later, they were playing football again when he noticed that Phil was sitting on a bench, watching. He looked rather miserable. Then Mr Davidson was sitting and talking to him. Why?

The answer came out later, over cocoa. They'd talked to his parents over the phone, and Phil had asked to go home, even though it was only Wednesday. There'd be one less in Simon's tent tonight, one less friend to swap stories and jokes with. He didn't know what to think. He'd thought the accident would all be over when they got back to camp, and it hadn't been. The accident was going on and on. They'd told Phil's parents, so they'd have to tell his own parents as well. They'd have to tell the people back at school. They'd have to tell Mr Burroughs, the Head. It was like he'd thrown a stone into the centre of a massive lake, and the ripples were spreading further and further away and he couldn't stop them now.

He'd said sorry. He'd said it *lots* of times that day to *lots* of people, but it hadn't made the injury go away, and it wouldn't buy back that afternoon sitting in the hospital waiting room. 'Sorry' wouldn't bring Phil back to camp, either. 'You can't turn the clock back', as his mum used to say, 'and you can't make time stand still. You can only go forward'. Simon wasn't sure what that meant, but he didn't feel like making any hard tackles tomorrow.

❖

Thinking time

We can't go back in time to change the silly things we've done in the past. But we can learn from our mistakes and try not to do it again in future. Can you think of silly or dangerous things you've done that now make you feel embarrassed?

What can you learn from what happened to you? Is there any way you can change what you're doing now, to stop it happening in future?

Prayers

Father God, when I think of that silly thing I did, it makes me feel all horrible inside, and I don't think I can change that. Show me how to sort things out.

If I have to say sorry to someone, show me how to do it so that it means something real. I am sorry. Help me to learn from this so it doesn't happen again. And help me to forgive myself too, so I don't keep going on and on about it. Amen

Father God, when I play, I want to win. Help me to remember that it's only a game and not a war. It's important, but it's not that important. Amen

Thinking time activity

People can sometimes feel very guilty when they hurt someone—but never do anything to sort it out. Those feelings can last for a very long time. Have you ever hurt someone like that, on purpose or by accident? Do you still think about it?

Why not try to sort it out? Create a 'Sorry' card for the person you have hurt, which shows that you know it was painful and you really wish them all the best in the future. (It may be helpful to discuss this with an adult, so that you can do it really well.) When you give the card to the person, spend some time with them to show that you really mean it.

✪ **First Aid is about knowing what to do (and what *not* to do) when someone has an accident. (Would *you* know what to do if you came across someone who had fallen down the stairs?) The St John Ambulance service provide a whole range of courses for people of any age to learn about First Aid. Why not find out more from your local branch? You could even end up *saving a life* one day!**

Medicines
and drugs

Anyone who belongs to Christ is a new person.
The past is forgotten, and everything is new.

2 Corinthians 5:17

What does it mean to live a *full* life? Jesus said he had come to bring life to people in the best possible way, and that includes enjoying being yourself as God made you. Some people need help from medical science to live a full life, but that can be difficult. Imagine having to take a pill or have a regular injection just so that you can live normally! Some people find that hard to understand—but the pills or other treatments from a doctor can make a real difference to someone's life. See what Declan discovers here.

Gravity

It was *that* time again. He didn't like it, but he knew it had to happen.

'Declan!' called Miss Acton. 'It's time!'

He grabbed a drinks bottle from his own tent, then hurried over. Mr Davidson was coming too. He always had to be there as well.

'Here it is,' she said, holding out the pill. Declan took it and stuffed it in his mouth. It didn't have a taste, but he still didn't like the idea of having to take a pill, although he knew he had to take it. He had a few swallows of drink to wash it down.

'You don't like taking them, do you?' she commented.

Declan shook his head. 'The others say I'm a druggie.'

Mr Davidson frowned. He'd have to do something about that, but not this minute. 'They're wrong,' he said. 'Drugs are what some people use to run away from their problems. These pills *do* help you, don't they?'

Declan gave him a look that showed he wasn't sure, but he gave a polite thank you, and then ran off to find the others by the dining room. He had to have a pill before every meal. Miss Acton wrote down the time it was given in a little book and signed it, then Mr Davidson signed it as well.

'He's doing really well!' she said, putting the book away.

Mr Davidson agreed. Declan had to take a special pill three times a day to stop him from being hyperactive. If he didn't take the pill, then his mind started racing, he would start to fidget, and he couldn't keep his mind on anything for more than thirty seconds. He could also lose his temper amazingly quickly. No one knew why he was like it, but the pill helped him to cope with school. Since starting to take it, he was actually making a lot of progress, especially in Maths. It was something to do with stimulating the bit of the brain that helps you to concentrate on things.

'Will he have to be on those pills for the rest of his life?' asked Miss Acton.

Mr Davidson shrugged. He wasn't a doctor. 'Who knows? I'm just glad he's got them. There was a week in school when he didn't have the pills, and on some afternoons the only thing I could get him to do in class was to sit with a book on a rocking chair. I brought the chair in from home, just to see if he would sit still in something that moved.'

Other people and their attitudes can be a real problem for people taking medication, or for people who have to use aids like a wheelchair or a hearing aid. Why do you think that is?

Other children have said...

'...because they don't like them because they are different...'

'...because some people like being horrible to others...'

'...because they pick on them...'

80

After the meal, it was time to tackle the indoor climbing wall. It was built inside a long brick shed. The whole length of the wall was covered in large sections of painted wooden board, with strange little bits of rock fixed to them. These were the places to put your hands and feet, as you traversed the wall—or rather, climbed sideways along it. It wasn't very high, but it was very long—about thirty metres.

Once they were all wearing helmets, Mr Williams sat them down and explained how it worked.

'Now then, this is called "bouldering". The idea is to get from one end of the wall to the other. When you're climbing, try to keep most of the strain on your leg muscles. Don't get too high—if you fall off, then you can just climb on again from that point until you reach the end.'

Soon, two lines of children were standing at the middle of the wall, then starting to climb off to the left and right, one by one. Some fell off after traversing only a metre of wall, but it was fun, and they all tried to keep going. The ones who were thinner seemed to be better at it, but then Gemma had a go, and nearly went the whole length, which surprised everybody! She seemed to be incredibly flexible, despite being a little podgy.

'She's *thinking* her way across,' said Mr Williams. Miss Acton saw Gemma stopping, looking for the next few handholds, then making the traverse, a few holds at a time. 'She's good, isn't she?' She was—the best so far.

Has somebody you know ever surprised you with what they can do?

Other children have said...

'Yes, my dad surprised me when he did the splits!'

'Yes, my mum, when she showed me she can hold her breath for a long time under water!'

Then it was Declan's turn on the wall. He'd never done anything like this before, apart from climbing a few trees near home. This wall looked… interesting. It was like a puzzle waiting to be cracked. He began. Stretch up, stretch across, grab the hand-hold, then swing the leg—he was there. Yes! He looked ahead. Yes, he could do it. Stretch up, swing again, and he'd done it. Whoops! It was the wrong foot. He swapped his feet over on the

rock, then looked ahead again. Yes, he could see where to go. It was as if he was thinking with his whole body. That's funny, he thought as he slid from handhold to handhold. It's like I'm working my way into the puzzle and out the other side. He reached the far end, and jumped down. Nobody noticed, because everyone else was either climbing or talking about it. Soon, the whole class had finished, and sat waiting for the next challenge.

'Now we're going to up the stakes a bit!' said Mr Williams. 'We'll start at the far ends of the wall, working our way along towards the centre. But this time, if you fall off, then you'll have to leave it and join another line to start again from either end.'

They began. Soon, it was Declan's turn. This bit of wall was different, with smaller handholds, some spread much further apart. That didn't matter, he thought, studying the gaps. I just have to put my weight on a smaller point, and stretch further. He worked out where his legs needed to go, then began, swinging, pausing, twisting up and down, all his muscles working together.

Some of the class started to notice. 'DEC-LAN! DEC-LAN!' someone shouted, and others joined in. Swing, stretch, pause, look—he was in a rhythm now, thinking with his hands and feet. It was as if he was defeating gravity. He reached the end and everybody cheered!

'That was fantastic!' said Mr Williams. 'You're a natural climber!'

Declan didn't know what to say. Nobody had ever said he was a natural *anything* before, apart from being a nuisance. As he sat down, the others were patting him on the back and saying 'well done'. This was weird. He was a natural climber?

It's great to discover that you have a talent for something. Have you discovered *yours*, yet?

Other children have said...

'...yes, with my swimming...'

'...yes, with my story writing...'

'...yes, when I perform magic tricks...'

When it was Declan's turn again, he decided to be different. 'Can I do it one-handed?' he asked. He traversed the whole wall end to end, using only two feet and one hand, the other held behind his back all the time. Some of the class stared in amazement as he clambered past them. How was he doing it? After that, he asked, 'Now can I do it backwards?' Declan traversed the whole wall again in the opposite direction, this time with his *back* facing the wall for the *whole climb*.

'I've never seen it done like that before!' said Mr Williams in awe. 'Did you know you could do this?' Declan smiled, shaking his head. He really hadn't known at all. Then he had a race with Gemma, both starting from opposite ends to see who could reach the centre first. She was good, but Declan won, with everybody cheering and Gemma smiling as well. It had been a good contest.

As they were walking back to the tents, Declan's head was in a whirl. He was a natural climber! He was good at something! No, he was *really* good at something, better than anyone he knew, and he hadn't known it.

Was it the pills doing it? No. The pills were *allowing* him to do it, allowing him to think and work things out for himself. He had the power in him anyway, and the pills were helping him to use it. They weren't drugs. They were helping him to *live*.

Some people can become dependent on things like alcohol or drugs when they misuse them. That means that they first started taking them because it made them feel good. The trouble is, if you *keep* taking these things on a regular basis, your body gets so used to it that it starts feeling sick when it *isn't* getting the stuff. You can't live without it. This is called addiction, and it can be very hard to stop being an addict. People often need a lot of help to free themselves from the habit—so don't start!

This is very different from the sort of medicine that Declan has, because his was prescribed for him by a doctor, and it's there to help him live his life normally. Doctors are the only people with the training to know this, so *never* mess about with medicines, including those prescribed for other people. *Always follow a doctor's instructions* if you ever have to take them!

❖

Thinking time

What are the best things for you about being alive?
- Think of all the things you like to do.
- Think of all the things you can listen to, or see, or smell, or touch, or taste.

Father God, thank you that I am alive! Thank you for all the amazing things around me. Thank you that I'm still discovering things about myself even now. I don't know my future, but you are going to be there to share it with me. Thanks again. Amen

Father God, I don't like taking medicine. Sometimes it doesn't taste nice, and I wish I could be like everyone else who doesn't have to take it. Help me to be thankful for it. Thank you that there are enough doctors in this country to sort out everyone who needs help. Please let there be more doctors for those places in the world where it's not that easy. Amen

Thinking time activity

Using an encyclopedia or other reference materials, find out about a medical condition that affects someone you know and care about (or even yourself). Possible topics are diabetes, epilepsy or asthma. Has the treatment changed over the years, as scientists make new discoveries? Ask an adult to help you access websites devoted to that subject. You never know what you might discover! Use your findings to create a booklet about that medical condition.

Why not get involved in fund-raising for a medical charity like RNIB (Royal National Institute for the Blind) or something similar? You could help to pay for real scientific research or medical care!

Healthy friendships

Our tongues are small, and yet they boast about big things. It takes only a spark to start a forest fire!

James 3:5

Love is kind and patient, never jealous, boastful, proud, or rude. Love isn't selfish or quick-tempered. It doesn't keep a record of wrongs that others do. Love rejoices in the truth, but not in evil. Love is always supportive, loyal, hopeful, and trusting.

1 Corinthians 13:4–7

Boys and girls start to 'notice' each other from the age of around nine or ten, but everyone is slightly different. It's all part of our natural development from children to adults, and our feelings can be rather strange as our bodies adjust and develop. It doesn't help when we see or read stories on TV or in books or magazines that are all about 'falling in love'. See the trouble that Stephanie and Paula stir up in this story when *they* get too worked up about it!

It'll all end in tears

The two girls were howling with laughter. Mr Davidson had to know why, so he asked.

'It's a game we're playing,' said Stephanie. 'We ask people these twelve questions, and then we tell them what they're really thinking.'

'We tell them who they *really* love!' added Paula. 'Can we try it on you, Mr Davidson?'

Mr Davidson could sense trouble heading towards him like a runaway lorry.

'No, thank you, not in a million years! What sort of questions do you ask?' They showed him their list. Most of the questions were the sort that asked you to name the first thing in your head when somebody said a certain word. 'Where did you get all this?' he asked.

'From a magazine,' replied Stephanie. 'We've been trying it out on the boys. It's so funny!'

Mr Davidson felt a sinking feeling in his stomach, and groaned. Yes, it was 'boyfriends and girlfriends' time again. Why did it always start with the girls? As a boy, he remembered playing 'kiss chase' at primary school playtime and kissing Susan Ranger, but that was a long time ago. Come to think of it, the girls had started that game too.

'Can't you two find something a little more interesting to do—like climbing trees?' The look they gave him said 'no'. He made a mental note to remember to make sure that the school nurse came in soon to give the class their 'growing up' talks.

'It'll all end in tears,' he warned. He wondered whether to ban them from doing it, but thought not. You can't ban *everything* that could turn out bad. If you did, children would never be allowed out.

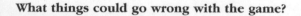

What things could go wrong with the game?

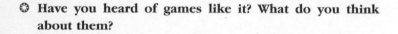

Other children have said...

'...someone could do it on them and they won't like it...'

'...things could be spread...'

'...people may get embarrassed and cry...'

'...someone's feelings could be hurt...'

○ **Have you heard of games like it? What do you think about them?**

After tea time, Stephanie and Paula came to see him. Both were limping. 'Brian *kicked* me!' Stephanie wailed. 'He went and pushed Paula over as well!'

Mr Davidson sipped his coffee. 'How did it start?' He knew what she was going to say next.

'We did the quiz with Brian, then we told him what he was thinking, and then he kicked me and pushed Paula!'

'Did he look really angry?'

'Yes,' she sniffed.

'Which bit of the quiz made him angry?'

Stephanie now looked a little embarrassed, as if, all of a sudden, she wanted to be somewhere else.

'Umm... er... we told him who it was he fancied.'

'I see. And who was that?'

There was another pause, and then an answer. 'Miss Acton.'

'So, you told him that he was in love with his teacher. Were you laughing a bit when you said this?' He gazed at their guilty expressions. 'Yes, I think you were. So why do you think he kicked you?'

After a pause, she spoke. 'Because he was embarrassed.'

'Yes. Kicking and pushing's always wrong, but you've been kicking his feelings, haven't you? Boys don't always like to talk about what's deep inside, and they hate having it dragged out of them like you just did. At his age, I might have felt like kicking you as well. Oh, and how do you think *Miss Acton* would feel about all this? She's over there now. Would you like me to call her over?'

'NO!' they declared, shocked at the thought.

What do you think Miss Acton would have to say about all this?

Other children have said...

'...she could be embarrassed...'

'...she could just laugh...'

Well *you'd* better sort this all out with Brian before I have to. I think you'd better convince him that you're sorry before Miss Acton hears about it, don't you?'

They nodded, and trudged away towards the football field. Funny, that—they weren't limping now. Mr Davidson sighed. It seemed so much easier when he was at primary school. Then he thought about Susan Ranger again. No, come to think of it, those feelings were never easy to handle when you were growing up. Brian was obviously very angry. 'Love' was a lot more complicated than the girls had realized, and they had hurt him by turning it into a joke.

✤

Thinking time

Romantic love is just a feeling—and, like every feeling, it comes and goes. Real love is much more than this—if you look at the list from 1 Corinthians 13, it's clear that love is something you *choose* to do for someone else, even when life is tough. The love that's talked about in the Bible is a lot deeper than anything you'll see on a TV soap.

Think of the names of some people who have loved you. Look at the list from 1 Corinthians again. Which kinds of love did those people show you?

Prayers

Father God, thank you for love. Thank you for all those people who have ever shown any kind of care for me. Help me to learn from their example, and to learn to love others in the same way. Amen

Father God, as I grow up, I will see and hear all sorts of messages about what 'love' is. Help me to remember what you say about real love, so I can tell the good messages from the bad ones. Amen

Thinking time activity

Create a poster using the Bible passage about love from 1 Corinthians 13. (It's a bit longer than the extract quoted at the beginning of this story.) Think about how you could illustrate some of these ideas, with cut-out pieces of newspaper or magazine, cartoons, or something else. Be creative!

Disability, co-operation and leadership skills

[The Pharisees] are like blind people leading other blind people, and all of them will fall into a ditch.

Matthew 15:14

All I know is that I used to be blind, but now I can see!

John 9:25

Millions of people in the world succeed in living their lives despite blindness, deafness, and a whole range of other medical problems. Most disabled people don't want sympathy—they just want to be allowed to get on with their lives like everyone else, without other people making their lives harder by having unhelpful attitudes. Jesus told us to love our neighbours as we love ourselves, and you probably know someone with a disability. Have you ever wondered how it affects them? Why not ask them?

This story is about blindness. Blind people don't have super-sensitive hearing or touch to help them get about—they just have to use these other senses more. In this story, some children get a chance to discover a little about what it's like to be blind—and also find out about something else.

The sensory trail

'Right then,' said Mr Buechner, 'Would you kindly sit down in a circle on the grass. Then, each of you remove one of your trainers, and put them in a pile in the middle.'

What? Taranjit did so anyway. There were eight children in the group, so eight rather beaten-up trainers soon lay in the middle of the circle. Mr Buechner stepped into the circle to explain the game.

'Now, to play this game, I want you to shut your eyes. I'm going to jumble up the trainers and give each one to different people. You've got to keep your eyes shut and pass the trainers round to your left. When your own trainer comes past, you can keep it, but you can only use your senses of smell and touch to identify it. See if you can do it! No cheating!'

Taranjit shut his eyes, and a trainer was placed in his hands. He smelled inside it. YUCK! The others were making disgusted noises as well, but they kept their eyes shut as the trainers went round the circle. How could other people's feet smell so foul? Wait a minute—that *particular* disgusting smell was familiar. Was it his trainer? Yes! He opened his eyes. The others had their trainers too. They had completed the task in just over one minute.

'Excellent!' said Mr Buechner. 'That was meant to give you a little introduction. This whole set of activities is designed to make you use your other senses instead of just relying on your eyes. Put your trainers on, then follow me into the woods.'

Most people share the five senses of sight, hearing, touch, taste and smell. Which of these have you used in the last few minutes?

Other children have said...

'...sight, when I was reading this...'

'...smell, when I went to the toilet!'

'...hearing, when my friend was talking to me...'

On arriving in the woods, they found themselves standing in a small clearing of short grass surrounded by trees. Mr Buechner opened a sack to produce a set of brown bags made of thick cloth, looking like pillowcases. He handed them out.

'Now then—in a minute, you're going to have to put one of these on each of your heads. I'm then going to lead each one of you by the hand to a tree. When you get there, I want you to hug the tree—or at least, I want you to feel it and get to know it just from touch. Once you're all in position, I'll start blowing a whistle at ten-second intervals. It's your job, then, to try to walk towards me with your blindfold on, making your way across the woodland floor using the sound of the whistle for directions. I'll keep blowing it, but you'll have to keep listening hard. Walk slowly, so that you don't hurt yourselves if you bump into anything. Got that? Hoods… ON!'

This must look really silly, thought Taranjit, as he stood there wearing a hood. He waited patiently until he heard Mr Buechner walk past, stop, then take him by the hand for a few metres until he was standing by a tree. 'We're there now, Taranjit. Reach out.' This was *his* tree! He felt the grooves and ridges of the rough bark.

'RIGHT THEN,' Mr Buechner called out a few minutes later from somewhere else. 'WOULD YOU ALL START WALKING TOWARDS ME!' The whistle blew. Taranjit started walking with little steps. The whistle blew again. Was that left or right? The ground felt uneven. He stopped, reached out—another tree! The whistle blew again—*that* way, round the other side of the tree. He made his way round it, then bumped into something soft that said 'OW!' That had to be David! Taranjit got past him, listening harder, then headed right as the whistle blew again. The ground was levelling out. What was that warmth on his hands? Sunshine! Yes! Nearly there!

Suddenly, his blindfold was removed by Mr Buechner. 'Well done!' he said.

Dazzled by the fresh sunlight, Taranjit was now standing in the middle of the clearing. Brian had already got there, and Declan, so he must have been the third to arrive. He could see David in the distance, tangled up in the low branches of a small tree and lifting up his blindfold, trying to cheat his way back, but Mr Buechner saw it and told him to try to do it fairly. The others were coming into the clearing now. When David finally arrived, he said it 'wasn't fair', but Mr Buechner congratulated them all.

'Well done! Now you've got a little idea of what it's like to be blind, when people have to rely on hearing and touch to know where they are. I wonder if you can find the tree where you started from? Try to retrace your steps and identify it by touch.'

Was that what being blind was like? Taranjit retraced his steps, thinking about his great-great-grandmother, the one who sat in the corner at family parties and who asked if she could feel his face when they were introduced. She was 97, and almost completely blind now. It had felt a little creepy to see this little old lady hunched up in the corner of the room, and to have her fingers touching your hair, but Taranjit understood now why she did it. There was no other way to get a sense of how big he was. 'My, how you've grown!' she'd always say.

Do you know someone who is blind or partially sighted? What sorts of things do *they* have to do to cope with everyday life?

Other children have said...

'...my grandad is like that. When we are out together, he sometimes asks where we are...'

'...my gran is losing her sight. When we walk together, I have to be careful to tell her if there is something she could trip over...'

Taranjit scanned the edge of the woodland area. Where was his tree? Was it this one? It looked awfully big. He shut his eyes as he touched it, trying to remember the grooves and ridges. Yes!

'Hey! That's my tree!' said David, coming up behind him.

'No it isn't! Go and find your own!' Taranjit replied angrily. Typical!

David wandered off, grinning. He'd known it wasn't his anyway. He was just trying to get away with doing less—again. Taranjit used to laugh at his jokes back at school, but not now.

Mr Buechner called them back. 'Now it's the team challenge —the sensory trail. You're going to have to tackle an assault course together, completely blindfolded. You'll be following a rope, but it will be heading up, down, and in and out of a whole range of obstacles. The person at the front will have to explain to everyone else what's ahead, because he or she will be meeting it first. I'll swap the leader round from time to time so you'll all have a go. Would you all please line up, one behind the other, and put your blindfolds on.'

'Can I go at the front?' asked David, who liked to be first at everything.

'Yes, David,' he replied, '*when* it's your turn.' David made a face, but they all ignored him.

The children lined up, all wearing their hoods, and each placed a hand on the shoulder of the person in front. Brian was leader. Then they set off slowly, looking like a small herd of elephants, each clutching the tail of the one in front.

Would *you* like to be at the front of the line? How could you help the others following you?

Other children have said...

'...yes. I could tell them what's coming up...'

'...no. It'll be scary and I might bump into everything...'

Brian's hand was placed on the rope by Mr Buechner.

'Now Brian,' he said, 'you'll have to tell everybody else what's going on. Sometimes they'll have to swap hands or step to one side of the rope or the other, and *you'll* have to tell them to do it. Got that?' Brian nodded, and they were off.

'It's going down!' he said, and the others followed. 'OW!'

That was Brian hitting something. 'It's a tunnel! We're going into a tunnel! Keep your heads down!' It was working so far. They crawled through on hands and knees, then stood up on the other side. 'We're going over some holes,' he called out. 'AAARGH!' That was Brian going down again, but then he called out, 'They're car tyres! Everyone, have you got that? They're only tyres! Be careful where you put your feet!' Bit by bit, they all made their way over.

Then it was time for a change of leader. David took over. 'We're going over some steps!' he shouted. 'OUCH! That hurt!'

'Slow down, there's no hurry!' said Mr Buechner, who must have been nearby. The group clambered over the steps, then carried on following the rope. 'IT'S A BRIDGE!' cried out David. Taranjit heard a splash up ahead. 'UUURGH! MY FEET ARE ALL WET!' David wailed.

'Taranjit, would you take over, please?' asked Mr Buechner. 'David, I told you not to dash on. Enjoy the frogs!' There was the sound of dripping water and *a lot* of moaning, as David was led out and put at the back of the line again. His shoes were now making squishy sounds as he walked.

Taranjit was leader! He froze. He was on the bridge! It was bouncing up and down a bit, and he couldn't see! He panicked. 'I'm stuck!' he exclaimed.

Gemma was behind. 'No you're not!' she said. 'Feel your way ahead with your feet! Come on! You can do it!' Taranjit held on to the swaying rope and inched his way forward, hoping the bridge was strong. It felt just like a plank of wood. 'Come on, everybody!' he called out, trying not to sound afraid (even though he was). How high was it? How deep was the water? He kept edging forward, feeling his way with his feet. Firm ground! 'It's all right! We're at the end!' he called out.

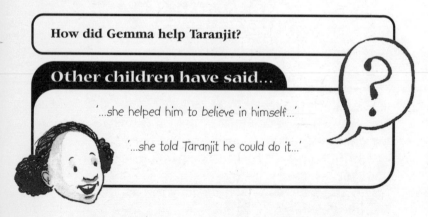

How did Gemma help Taranjit?

Other children have said...

'...she helped him to believe in himself...'

'...she told Taranjit he could do it...'

The course wasn't over yet. The rope led them further on. All of a sudden, there was a horrible clatter and Taranjit almost squeaked in fright. It was a noisy moving barrier of some sort. 'We're going through something, everybody!' he yelled. 'Don't worry! Just keep going!' Once they were through, Gemma took over, and Taranjit was placed behind David, who was jerking and jumping. 'What's wrong?' he whispered.

'Nothing,' said a miserable voice that clearly meant there was something wrong.

'It can't be much further!' Taranjit replied, trying to make David feel better. The course led them around trees, over more barriers, and then into another tangle of posts and ropes.

At the end, Mr Buechner removed their hoods. Light! All of a sudden, they could see again! Where were they now? It was a completely different area.

'Well done!' said Mr Buechner. 'Now go back following the rope, and *see* all the things you went through!' They did. It was amazing. The bridge was only about twenty centimetres above the water, which was actually only a long, deep, muddy puddle about five centimetres deep. The clattery barrier was just loads of plastic bottles hanging on string above the rope. The buried tyres looked so easy to cross. Did Brian fall over *that*?

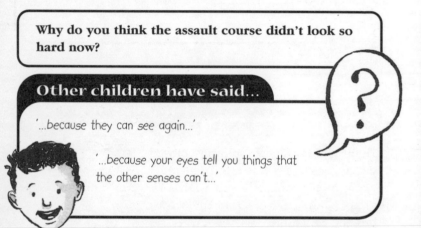

Why do you think the assault course didn't look so hard now?

Other children have said...

'...because they can see again...'

'...because your eyes tell you things that the other senses can't...'

Soon they were back at the beginning with Mr Buechner. 'Well done to all of you,' he said. '*That's* what it's like to be blind, but it's also what it's like to be a leader of a group of people. When you're in charge, you might not have much more clue than anyone else about what to do—but it's your job to make sure that everyone is all right, and if you can give them a clue about what's coming next, and encourage them, then that's even more helpful.'

They headed back to the camp. The sensory trail had been weird. Taranjit had learned a little about being blind, but there was something else too. Being a leader could be rather scary—but he wanted to try it again.

Do you think that's a good picture of what it takes to be a leader? What qualities do *you* think someone needs to be a leader of other people?

Other children have said...

'...I think a good leader directs others...'

'...I think a good leader helps and warns the others...'

Thinking time

Think of the last meal you really enjoyed. Which senses did you use to enjoy it? Think hard about how you were able to see, hear, touch, taste and smell. Imagine eating the meal without each of these senses in turn. How would it have been different?

Prayers

Take a piece of chocolate, or another favourite food. Look at it closely for a minute, and smell it. Then taste it, enjoying the flavour for as long as you can. Then pray this prayer.

Father God, I live in an amazing world of sights and sounds, of things to touch and smell and taste. Thank you that you made this world for us to enjoy. This bit tastes so good! Amen

Father God, I can only imagine what it is like to be blind or deaf, or have some other disability. Help me to understand a little of what it's like, so I can be a friend to a disabled person when they need it. Amen

Thinking time activity

Get a sheet of newspaper. Your task is to tear it to make the shape of an elephant, but with your eyes shut. Have a look at what you made afterwards. Think about what this tells you about the way you use your eyes. (This makes a great party game, by the way!)

Changes at puberty

You are the one who put me together inside my mother's body, and I praise you because of the wonderful way you created me.

Psalm 139:13–14

Children grow up quickly, but it's hard to see that when it's happening to you. Some signs of growth are easy to spot—like the normal clothes that don't fit you as they used to, or the height chart with little marks showing where you were *last* year. But there are other changes as well, and they can be disturbing when you don't know what's going on.

She's dying!

Gemma was worried about Lottie. She'd been looking strange ever since they came to camp. They were sharing a tent because they'd asked to be together with Sarah, but Lottie seemed to be in a bit of a mood, all the time. When it came to settling down on the first evening, Gemma didn't know whether to ask if something was wrong.

'Oh, just leave her alone,' said Sarah. 'She's in a grump!'

Sarah had turned over and gone to sleep, but when there was all that *awful* business from the other tent with Jackie crying out about keys (which had woken everyone up except Sarah), Lottie had started crying to herself.

'What's wrong?' asked Gemma, giving her a hug.

'I don't *know*!' sobbed Lottie. 'I just feel… so… fed up!'

'Are you feeling homesick? I thought you'd been away before, with the Brownies and Guides!'

'I don't know!' replied Lottie. Gemma left it there, and they settled down eventually.

☺ **Do you sometimes feel sad for no apparent reason? When?**

Next day seemed to be better, although Lottie seemed to get really tired on the long walk. (Sarah had fallen in the stream and screamed in delight.) When they got back, Lottie just went back to the tent and fell asleep. This wasn't like her. Normally, she'd be

up and bouncing in five minutes, but she had to be woken for tea time.

'Oy! Sleepy-bones! Wake up!' called Sarah, pulling the sleeping bag off Lottie. Lottie muttered something unpleasant in return. Yes, she was in a mood!

On Tuesday evening, there was the climbing wall, studded with funny little bits of coloured rock. Gemma hadn't done any climbing before, but she had strong hands and strong legs. Soon, she was smoothly traversing several metres of wall in

one go, like a great spider. Everyone was *very* impressed! Mr Williams had set them all the target of getting along the whole length of the wall without dropping, and Gemma had done it! She normally didn't enjoy PE very much (especially if it involved running), but this was different. Everyone cheered when she finished a last section of wall and jumped down, but when she sat with the others, she saw that Lottie was finding it all rather hard. In fact, she seemed to be giving up almost at once.

'This is stupid!' she was saying to herself. 'I can't hold on!' She'd given up in disgust and went to sit down, taking off her helmet. She looked as if she would have thrown the helmet at the wall if none of the staff were watching. 'Have another go, lazy!' said Sarah, but Lottie just glared.

This wasn't like her.

When they settled down that evening, Gemma asked what was wrong.

'I told you *last night*! I don't *know*! Now *leave* it!' she said.

Gemma left her to sleep. Later, she heard Lottie crying quietly to herself, and gave her a hug. Lottie didn't pull away, but accepted it, almost curling into a ball inside her sleeping bag. This was weird. Before coming, they'd all talked about the mad things they were going to do at camp, but none of it was happening. Lottie wasn't homesick, but she didn't want to say what she was cross about. Was she ill? Gemma wondered. Perhaps they ought to have a word with Miss Acton in the morning.

What do you think is wrong?

Other children have said...

'...she's missing her home...'

'...she doesn't like being away from her mum...'

'...she's sick and upset...'

Next day, the class had been divided into two groups to take on different activities. One half went off to do the climbing wall, while Gemma, Sarah and Lottie's group set off to do some caving. First of all, they had to put on large over-suits that made them look like giant seals, then put on more helmets. Then they were taken to find the caving system which had been built underground on the other side of the site.

'I think you need to practise crawling!' said Mr Williams, and then the whole group was crawling across part of the field like a plague of overweight slugs. It was silly, but fun, and it got you warmed up. When they arrived, Mr Williams explained how the system worked, and the group were soon disappearing one by one into the cave mouth.

'I don't want to go,' said Lottie.

'You don't have to if you don't want to,' replied Mr Williams. 'Do you want to try just putting your head inside a little bit, and see what it is like?' She did. Then she tried putting her whole body inside. And then she scrambled outside again.

'I'm *not* going in there!' she said, looking pale.

'Scaredy-cat!' shouted Sarah, and disappeared into the cave. Gemma was amazed. She had seen Lottie do all sorts of weird and wacky things for a dare over the years. They'd had all sorts of adventures together. Why was Lottie now afraid of the dark? Was it the idea of being inside a tunnel? She didn't know.

'Do you want me to stay with you?' she asked. Lottie said nothing and frowned.

'*I'll* stay with her,' said Mr Davidson, who'd come along to watch. 'Go on, you go and explore.' Gemma did. It was great fun, but it would have been even more fun with Lottie. Afterwards, they all had to go for a shower and clean up, but it was then that Lottie started crying.

'Ouch! It really hurts!' she said, outside their tent as they were collecting their shower things.

'What hurts?' asked Gemma and Sarah.

'My belly!' She sat down, kneeling down and clutching herself, almost doubling up in pain. Sarah just stood there, panic-stricken.

What's the first thing you should do if someone falls sick?

Other children have said...

'...get someone who can help them more...'

'...get a responsible adult...'

'...make the person comfortable...'

'...you should get help and make sure that someone is with the person who is ill...'

Gemma thought quickly. 'Sarah! Get some help! I'll stay with her! Sarah?'

'What? Yes!' Sarah seemed to wake up, turned around, then sped off to the staff room where the teachers were having a coffee break.

'Mr Davidson! Miss Acton! Lottie's sick! She's dying!' They dropped their mugs and ran across to the camp, where Lottie was now curled up in a little ball inside her tent.

They sat her up, and asked a few questions. No, there was no headache. Yes, there was this cramp-like pain down there... and then Miss Acton asked another question to which the answer was yes. The teachers looked at each other, exchanged a few words, then Mr Davidson got up, and went over to sit on a bench. 'Gemma! Sarah!' he called. 'Would you come here for a minute?' He beckoned them over to come and sit with him.

What was going on? Wasn't this an emergency? Why had nobody phoned for an ambulance? Instead, Miss Acton had gone to her tent to fetch a bag. Soon, she was taking Lottie over to the showers.

'Tell me,' asked Mr Davidson, 'has Lottie been in pain for a long time?'

Gemma shrugged. 'I don't know. But she's been really grumpy and unhappy all week.'

'Does this mean she's not dying?' asked Sarah. She looked slightly disappointed at the way other people weren't dashing around in a panic like *she* was.

Mr Davidson bit his lip. 'It's all probably because she's just started her first period. Do you two know anything about periods?'

It was like a coin dropping in a slot machine. Gemma had been in on the lessons when the school nurse came to school, but she hadn't made the connection. She remembered all the stuff about eggs and tubes and wombs and all that... but she hadn't connected it all with Lottie. Of course!

'Is she all right?' asked Gemma.

'I'm sure Miss Acton will get her sorted out. We've been doing these camps for a few years now, and it had to happen that *somebody* would start their periods when we were here. It looks like this is the year!'

'Will she have to go home?'

'I don't see why. She's not sick, is she? We'll see how she gets on, and we'll phone home just to let her parents know, but if she can handle it, then great. It's different for each girl. Sometimes, the first one is the worst because it's not expected.'

'I *knew* it was periods! It had to be!' declared Sarah. Gemma and Mr Davidson exchanged a look which said a lot.

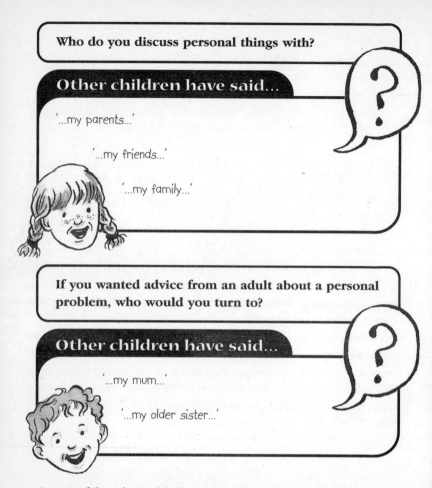

Who do you discuss personal things with?

Other children have said...

'...my parents...'

'...my friends...'

'...my family...'

If you wanted advice from an adult about a personal problem, who would you turn to?

Other children have said...

'...my mum...'

'...my older sister...'

Gemma felt rather odd discussing this with a man, but it was a rather strange day anyway, and she felt she could trust him.

'Will we be starting our periods soon, then?' she asked.

He shrugged. 'Who knows? For some girls it can be at age nine. For others, it can even be at fourteen or fifteen. It'll be when your body's ready. It's all about growing into the young woman you were meant to be, and your body will choose its own best time. Now, are you both all right? Sarah... you looked quite frightened when you dashed into the staff room.'

'Frightened? Me? Of course not!' Gemma and Mr Davidson exchanged another look.

Well, they seemed to be all right now. It was finally time to go and shower after the caving, so off they went. As Gemma got her shower kit, her teacher's words hung in her mind. 'The young woman you were meant to be.' That sounded rather nice. In a way, she was rather looking forward to it.

Did you know?

Boys and girls experience a lot of changes to their bodies at puberty.

Apart from increasing height and weight, boys become aware of these changes as they start growing more body hair (especially between their legs and under their arms), their testicles become larger, and their voices change, becoming deeper.

For girls, the development can seem more subtle. Their bodies grow more curvy, and they grow more body hair in the same places as the boys. But then there is the biggest change of all, which can begin nowadays at the age of nine—the beginning of periods. At the moment, about ten percent of girls start their periods at an age when they are still at primary school.

Periods are what happens when the body goes through the cycle of producing an egg and maintaining it in a warm, safe place for several weeks before disposing of it and creating another one. This natural process includes the flushing out of the old egg and the uterus lining—which produces a steady outpouring of blood which can last for several days. This is controlled by using tampons or pads which absorb the blood. For many girls, this can be a very emotional time—and it is sometimes painful. However, it's also a good sign that your body is working exactly as it should be as you slowly develop into a young woman.

❖

Thinking time

What are the things *you* look forward to about becoming an adult?

Are there any things you don't look forward to?

What responsibilities will you have to take on as you get older? These will increase from year to year, as you learn to take more important decisions that affect you. What sorts of things will you have to make your own decisions about, as you reach the ages of fourteen, sixteen, or eighteen?

Prayers

Father God, I'm unique. There's no one else like me in the whole world! You must have made me for a very special purpose. Help me to find out what that is over the next few years, and thank you for making me me. Amen

Father God, I don't like pain, and sometimes when I have a pain I want it to go away and it won't. I ask you to take it away and it's still there. Why? Please help me to cope with it, and please make it go away in the end. Amen

Thinking time activity

Find some good books about the changes that happen to boys and girls at puberty. Research what happens to you, then find out what happens to someone of the opposite sex. Make a list of any questions you have. Then find an adult to discuss them with, one whom you can trust to answer them well.

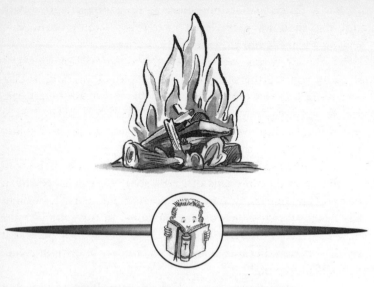

Postscript:
'The campfire'

First of all, there was that marvellous crackle you get when dry wood bursts into flame. The small twigs were burning hot enough to set the larger pieces alight now, and the flames were growing larger. Smoke began to rise. All around the clearing, the class were sitting down on logs to see the old miracle of fire coming back to life again.

They had heard about the campfire from other children who had come in previous years. Songs would be sung, and marshmallows melted and eaten. Long, terrifying ghost stories would be told by Mr Davidson, which *always* ended at a point you didn't expect, and *always* made you jump with fright.

Everything happened in the way it always did. That's what they liked about it.

But there was something more to do as the sky grew dark and the shadows grew longer—and the flames burnt low, leaving a mass of hot glowing coals.

Mr Davidson was speaking. 'I want you all to look up at the sky. Can you see the stars coming out? Now I'm going to take you on a journey, but you've got to keep looking. You see, you're not looking up. In space, there is no up or down. You're just nearer or further away from things. So you're not looking up. You're looking out.

'Keep looking. You're gazing out into space. The lights you see are great burning balls of gases, some of which have been burning for thousands, maybe millions of our years. Their light has taken years to reach us. In fact, some of the stars you see now may have burnt out, but we're still seeing their light as it reaches us now, because it started so far away and so long ago. Space is just so big!

'Each one of those stars is like our sun. It's a blazing hot explosion of gases and minerals. But do you know this amazing fact? You are made of the same stuff! The atoms that make up your body are made of the same kinds of material that built stars and moons and planets—you're just built in a different way. Each one of us here is totally unique. There's never been anyone else like you before, and there never will be anyone like you again.

'This week, you've learned a few more things about yourself, about what you *can* do—and maybe about what you still have to learn to do. But listen to me—don't *ever* say you are rubbish, or let anyone else say you are rubbish, because you aren't. You're all made of *stardust*! You were *all* made for a purpose! *Never* forget it!'

Mr Davidson had finished, but the whole class remained silent. Then a voice by the fire said what everyone else was thinking as they gazed out at the stars and the whole universe.

'Thank you, Lord.'

★ ★ ★ ★ ★ ★ ★

Stories to make you think

REF 1 84101 034 0, £3.99

Written especially for all those working or living with 6-10 year olds who find themselves needing to talk through topical and often sensitive issues, such as bereavement, bullying, family matters, spiritual awareness and self-value. Designed to stimulate discussion between adult and child, the stories are based mainly on real-life experiences and use biblical insights and thinking time to provide an accessible entry point into difficult subjects.

★ ★ ★ ★ ★ ★ ★

More stories to make you think

REF 1 84101 141 X, £4.99

Following on from the popular *Stories to make you think*, this book provides a further selection of topical and often sensitive subjects designed to stimulate discussion between adult and child. The author uses biblical insights and thinking time to provide an accessible entry point into diffcult subjects. Each story has been researched and tested in Circle Time and PSHE at primary level and can be used either in a one-to-one situation or with a group in the classroom, church or family.

★ ★ ★ ★ ★ ★ ★

Stories to help you pray

REF 1 84101 188 6, £4.99

Contains ten Bible stories, each told from the point of view of a child and followed by guided meditations. The stories are taken from the Gospel accounts and set within the correct historical and social background in order to enrich the child's understanding and to help the story to come alive. Key Bible verses are included.

The meditations are followed by directed questions to facilitate the child's experience of entering the story itself and an invitation to 'look out' of the story and take its meaning into the rest of the day. All the material has been thoroughly field-tested within the normal school day with 6–10s.